SERGIOMALEY

The Art of Etsy.

Sell like a monster.

Copyright © 2020 by Sergio Maley

All rights reserved. No part of this publication may be reproduced, stored or transmitted in any form or by any means, electronic, mechanical, photocopying, recording, scanning, or otherwise without written permission from the publisher. It is illegal to copy this book, post it to a website, or distribute it by any other means without permission.

First edition

This book was professionally typeset on Reedsy.

Find out more at reedsy.com

Preface

Etsy is a new market with potentially great sales and personal business growth. The knowledge that you will get longer in this book, use it to the fullest.

THE

Part One

In the first part of the book we will learn how to register, create professional lists, keywords and many other things a lot

complicated.

We will also practice, a lot of practice.

1

Knowledge and introduction

Etsy.com is a marketplace, new and still little known both in the world and in Italy. Little internal competition, which allows us to dominate the market of our niche, only we have to work on it.

This platform invests many millions of dollars in advertising and service improvement. Many vendors from around the world sell here, especially many of those who are engaged in **handmade products** and not only. Let's take a couple of examples: crafts, antiques and materials, unique limited edition products. These goods and other products are classified into a wide variety of categories such as art, photography, clothing, jewelry, food, cosmetics, toys and other accessories.

Great marketplace for various types of businesses that helps reach millions of buyers around the world.

Being a bit practical and smart, it can also be sold as " **dropshipping** », I will explain better how it can be done later.

This book is written in simple, conversational language with lots of theoretical things and lots of practice to do. I have written with detailed explanations to help you understand better and learn quickly.

Let's not waste time and start working on our shop without further delay, as time is money.

Make the most of the forces, possibilities and ideas that I will give you in this book to dominate the market.

2

REGISTRATION

Registration is very simple and does not take long, but there are some nuances.

Why are you opening a shop? Before opening a shop on Etsy, spending money, time and energy… ask yourself a question: why do I need it? And be completely honest with yourself.

Keep in mind even if the item you make is not unique, but you must have free time, desire and patience - welcome to the Etsy community!

If your products are unique and there is little competition, it will be much easier for you to succeed even with a minimal investment of time and effort. Well, if you want immediate results, but don't have the time or the desire to develop the store, then contact us on **www.sergiomaley.com** and we'll take care of it.

Let's begin!

We click on «Sign in» and a window pops out like in the image and then «Registration».

THE ART OF ETSY.

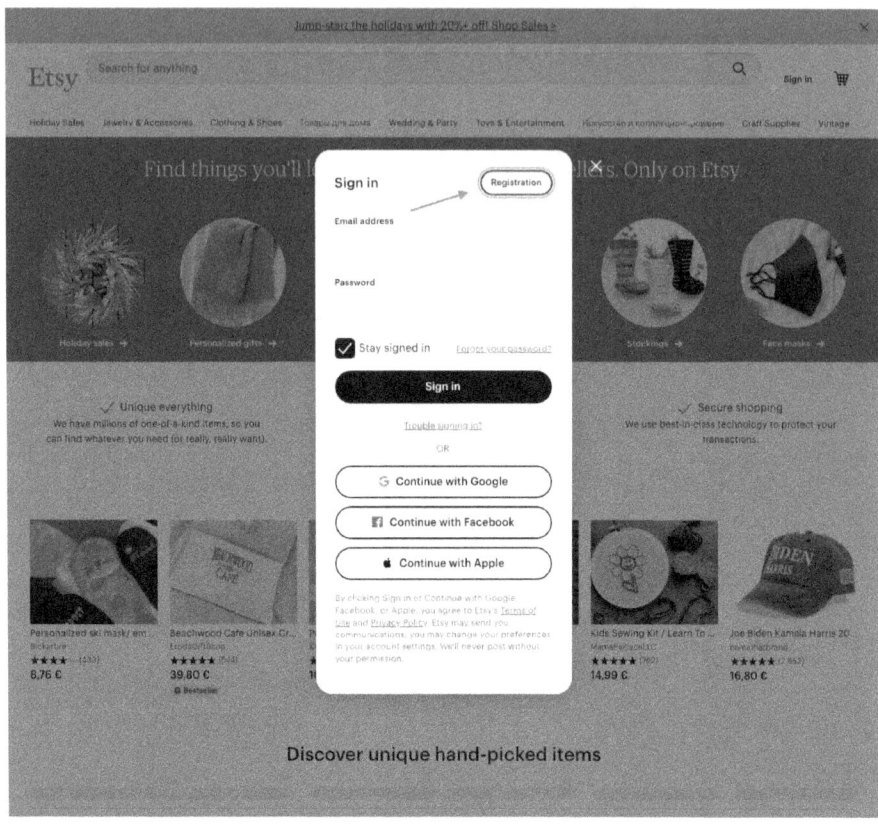

Next we find this window to insert Email, **First name (** not the store), Password and at the end
-> **Register.**

REGISTRATION

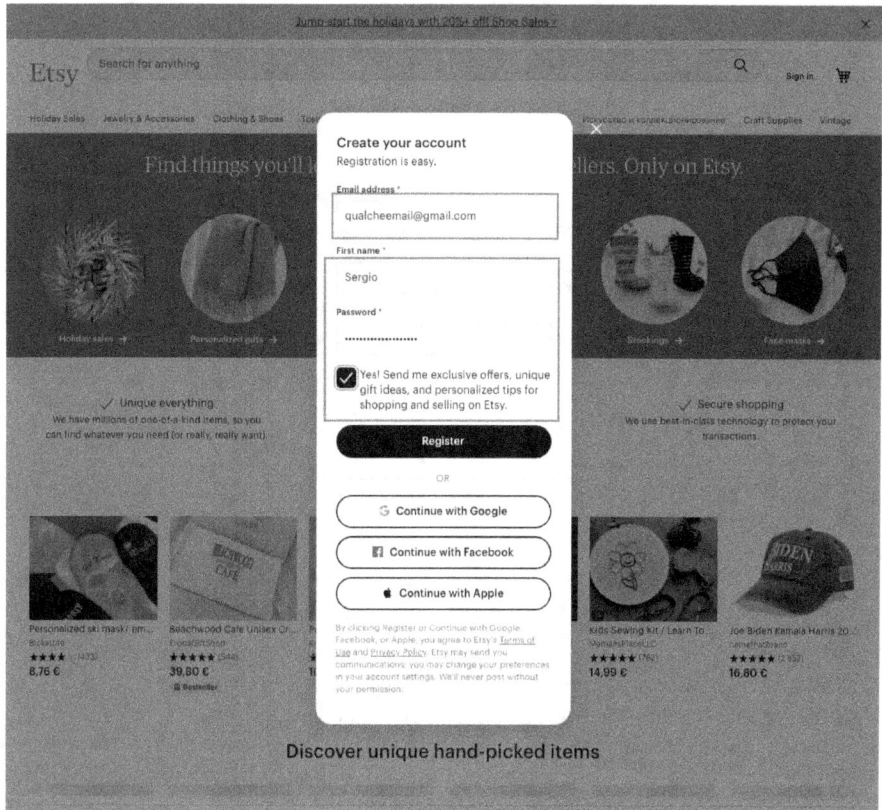

Okay, happy birthday huh! You are now registered on Etsy, but only as a buyer, not a seller. Go on. Now from the menu click on «You» and « **Sell on Etsy** "

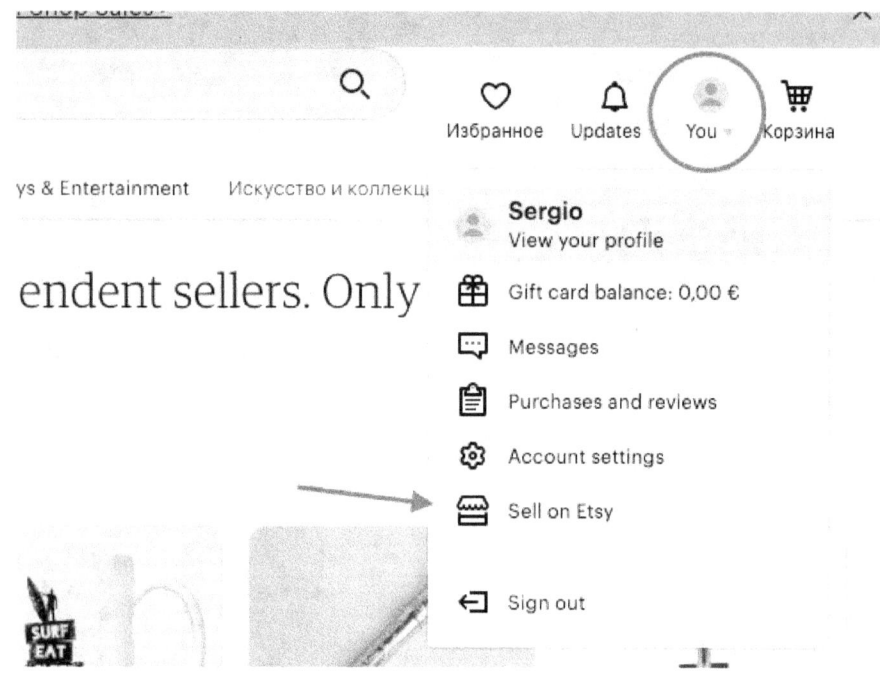

You'll find yourself with such an introduction page, but don't panic. Find
" **Open your Etsy shop** »And click on.

REGISTRATION

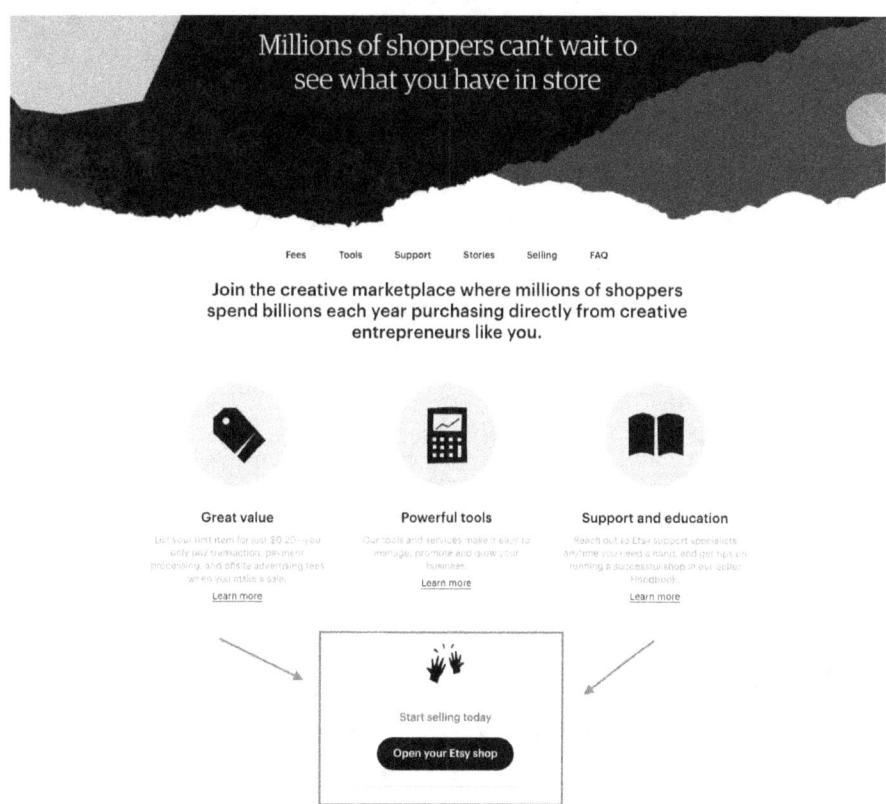

Set your shop preferences.

Now there are some things to do. select the language, country and currency of the store. Do we want to sell in the USA? well then, it means English (Choose the language of the shop in English (preferably, as Etsy is an English language site, so get Google Translate nearby, if you don't know this language)). Where do we sell from? In our case, this is Italy, you have to find it on the list. The currency is obviously the euro.

THE ART OF ETSY.

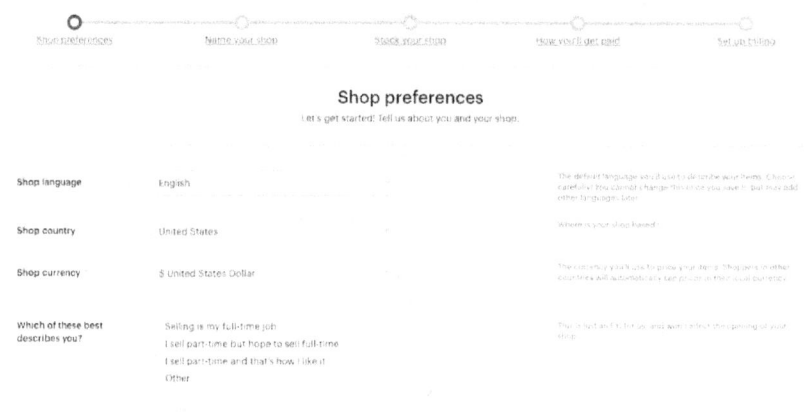

Choose the name of your Etsy shop.

It's time to name the shop. If your company already has a name, we enter it, otherwise we invent it. I recommend that you name a shop with roughly the same niche you will be selling in. For example, "SolarPowerBanksStore", "DogBandanas" has already been taken, so in our case it is "DogBandanasStore" - The niche of dog bandanas.

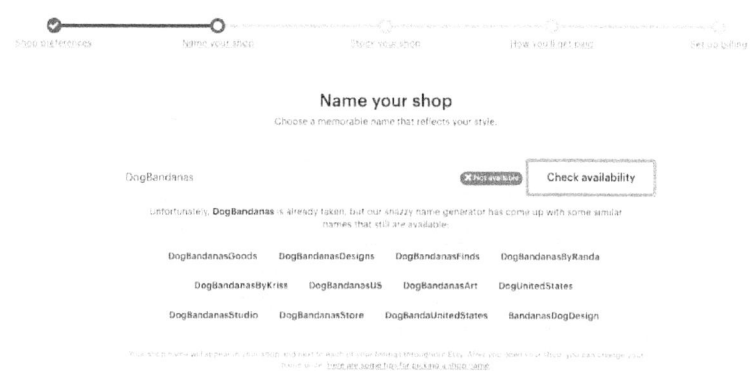

After assigning a shop name, Etsy asks us to add the first product. That said, the list of physical and digital items (think printable stationery, templates, stickers, gift tags) involves separate processes. We will show you the basics of how to list a tangible item; you can consult Etsy's help if you are placing a digital item.

Add photos.

Etsy recommends using at least five photos per item (you can include a maximum of 10) so that customers can see your product from various angles and that your images are at least 1,000 square pixels in size. Also, if you have variations of a product, such as a t-shirt with multiple colors, you can include photos for those variations so that customers can see all of their options.

Edit your thumbnail.

Your thumbnail is the first image of your item that your customers see in your shop, through search, and elsewhere on Etsy - think of it as the headshot of your product. Make sure it's good.

Complete the details of your ad.

Give your item a title that describes the product in as much detail as possible, considering your limit of 140 characters. You'll also have the option to provide an in-depth description, a bulleted overview of the product, and additional details such as the category and type of the product.

In the description section, you will also be able to preview your listing for a Google search result, which can help you optimize for ecommerce SEO.

Also, in the details of your listing, be sure to pay attention to the section titled "Renewal options". As we'll see about Etsy's rates below, if you select "Automatic," your listing will automatically renew after it expires, every four months. Each time the listing renews, you will be charged a fee of 0.20 cents, so you'll want to be sure to remember this when you start your shop.

If you prefer to renew the expired cards yourself or, alternatively, delete them, you can select "Manual".

Finally, you should take advantage of all 13 "tags" available per article. Buyers

REGISTRATION

they find your item by searching for keywords in the search bar, then work backwards and think about what a customer might type in the search to find your products. These keywords are what your tags should be. We will talk about SEO later.

Complete your inventory and pricing.

In this section, you will enter the product price, sales tax (if applicable), quantity (if you have more than one in stock), SKU number (if you have one) and variants. As mentioned above, you can add variations, such as sizes, materials, and colors, and link respective photos to those variations.

Set the shipping price.

Here you will include all the necessary details about your shipping processes, such as the shipping services you use, costs, country of origin, processing times, and the weight and size of the items.

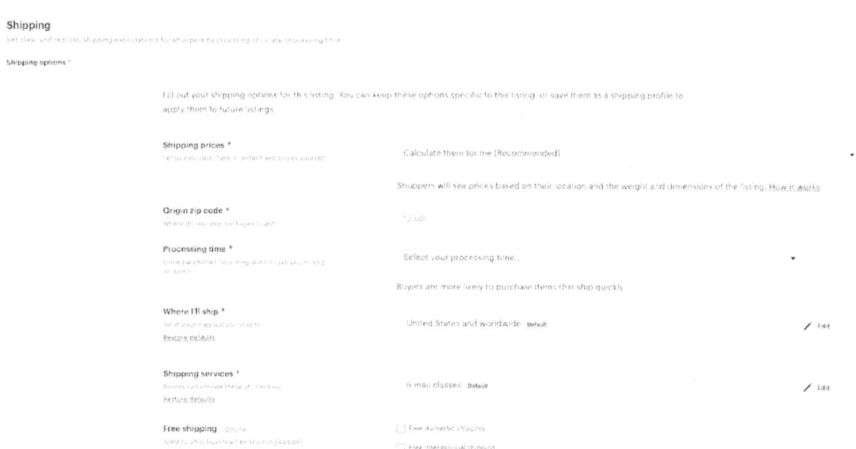

You can also opt for Etsy to calculate shipping prices for you (which they recommend). In this case, you will be prompted to enter the weight and dimensions of the item (when packed). Then, based on this information, you will be able to preview the shipping price that the buyer is seeing.

After you open your shop on Etsy, you will also have the option to set "Shipping profile" so you can quickly update items with the same shipping costs.

REGISTRATION

Post your ad.

You can preview the entire listing to see how it will appear to customers before publishing it.

When you first launch your Etsy shop, you can include as many listings as you like. Etsy recommends at least 10, as the more listings you have, the more likely customers are to find you.

That said, however, you'll want to remember that your listings aren't active until the setup process is complete, so you don't want to spend too much time on a large number of listings if you're looking to start memorizing quickly.

Choose your payment preferences.

Once you've added your items, you'll need to set up Etsy's payment preferences. First, choose how you prefer to accept payments - options include PayPal, check or money order, "other" or Etsy Payments, which is the primary way sellers get paid. You can accept credit cards, debit cards, Etsy gift cards, store credit, and more.

Currently, Etsy requires any eligible seller (based on their location) to offer Etsy Payments to do so. In this sense, although Etsy offered PayPal as a standalone payment option, starting May 15 2019, sellers in eligible countries, including the United States, must use Etsy Payments with integrated PayPal.

Also, if you are eligible for Etsy Payments, you will need to set it up as part of your payment settings, entering your bank account and home address (as shown above) to receive your payment deposits from Etsy.

Set up billing.

When starting an Etsy shop, this step will entirely depend on your country. In some countries, Etsy will require you to provide a credit card for identity authorization purposes. You'll also need a card on file so that Etsy can charge you sales fees (more info below).

If you are a capable seller, you have the option to sign up for automatic billing, in which case Etsy will automatically charge your credit card on file for the sales fees you incur, so you don't have to worry about paying your monthly reporting fees.

Open your shop.

At this point, you have successfully learned how to start an Etsy shop: after clicking on " **Open Your Shop** ", Your shop will be open.

Best wishes! :)

3

Store setup

Our shop was successfully opened. Now let's move on to customizing it and giving it the professional and quality look so that customers want to buy from you and only you.

Let's take for example a jewelry store (*the name of the shop I hid,*
for him not to advertising if maybe my book will make the success :), also to hide from the eyes "bad."
(If you are interested, write me on social networks, contacts
you will find in this book)). Take note, that the comments on the photos, I wrote in English, as I have great plans regarding this book, and translate it into many languages of the world. So much ... English is now our second language. Okay... let's proceed.

Add a bio and a photo (avatar).

Your public profile is how site visitors can learn more about you, both as an entrepreneur and as a person outside of your job.

In your bio you have free space to tell the audience pretty much anything you want. Talk a little about your background, your interests, yours

STORE CONFIGURATION

qualifications and tell the story behind your products, your mission and why love what you do. **But I would recommend writing your own niche keywords.**

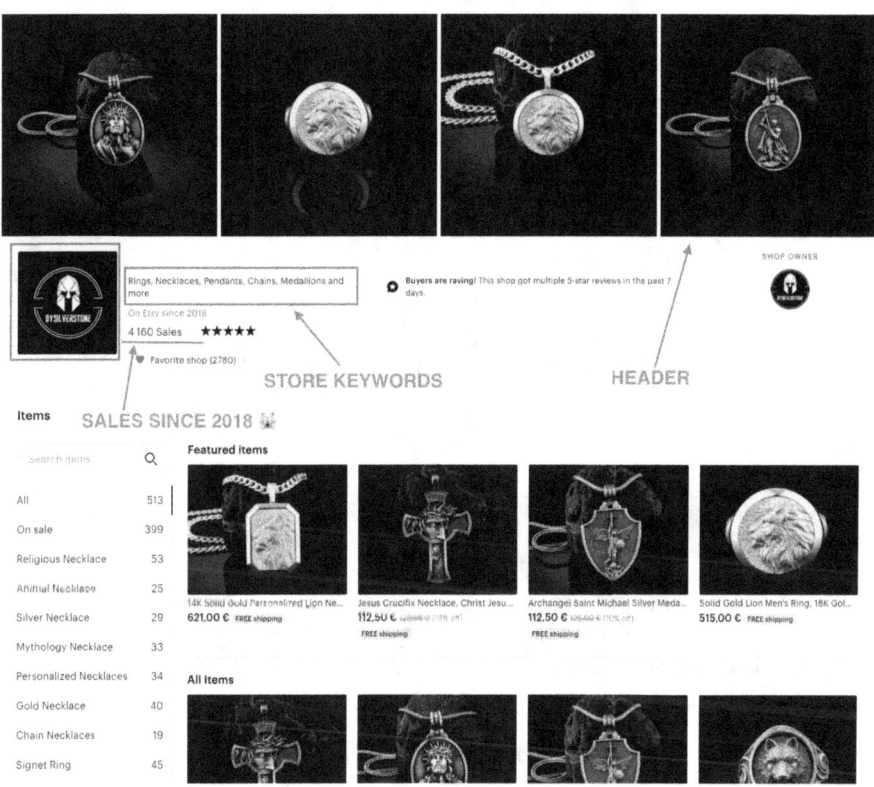

The profile photo must be 500x500 px for excellent quality, it is important that the photo is not ours: D, but it must be a logo. You can easily and effortlessly create it on **www.canva.com**

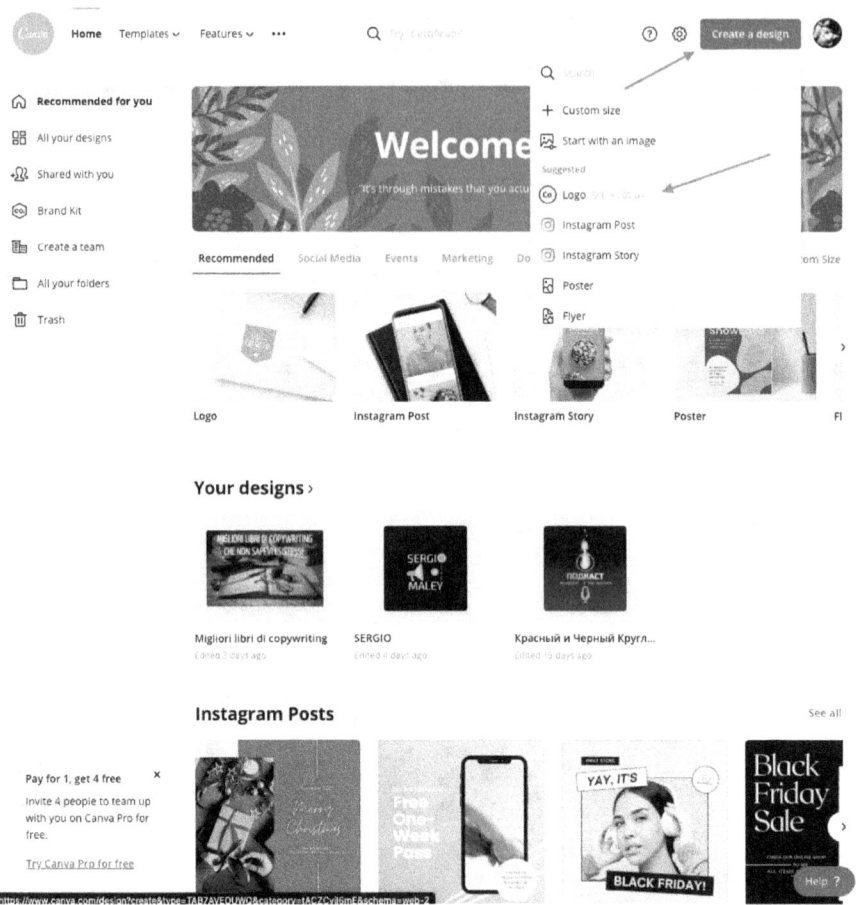

After that, you can select many ready-made templates, make some changes or create your own. After all this, click on Download and choose the format between .png and .jpg

STORE CONFIGURATION

Create your store header.

Header gives you the opportunity to decorate your shop and give it a professional look. The header should be of good quality, preferably with your shop name. If you have important discounts or announcements, you can also write them. The important thing is not to make it an advertising banner.

THE ART OF ETSY.

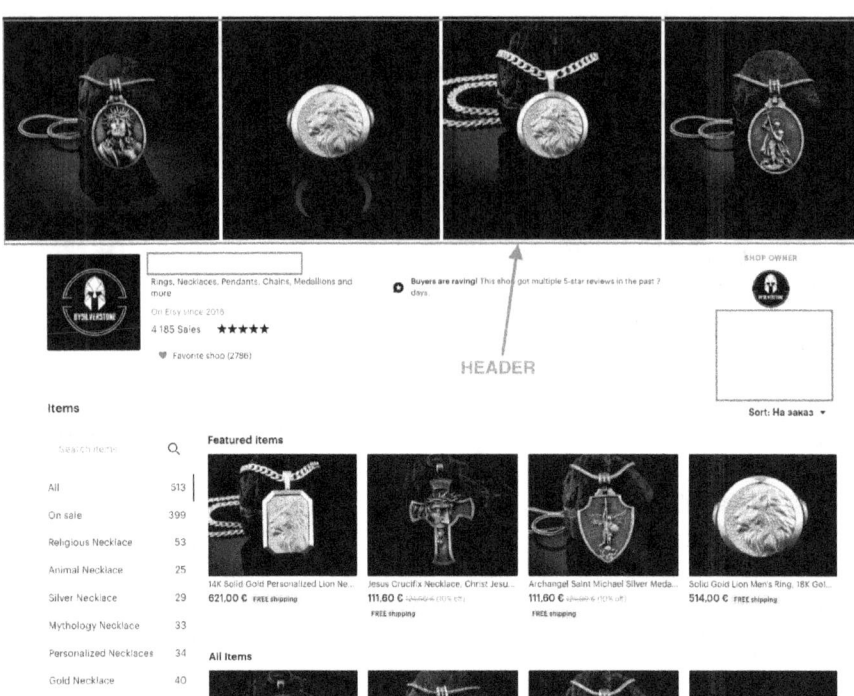

Example 1.

STORE CONFIGURATION

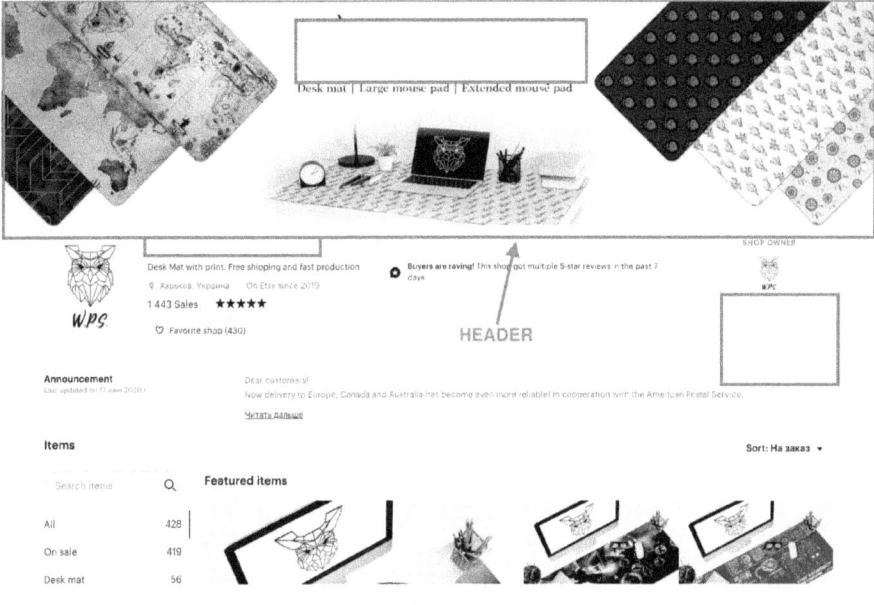

Example 2

For this there is a special section called "Announcement". Describe your ad as well as possible, including the keywords of what you sell.

Announcement

Set your policies.

Here you will answer any relevant questions your customers may have about your manufacturing, processing, shipping and payment processes. Be sure to include an estimate of the processing and shipping time so your shoppers have a clear idea of how long their items will take to reach them.

Also, be sure to include your return and exchange policy and the payment methods you accept. If you have indicated "other" in your payment settings, you will need to include information and instructions on this payment method in this section and on each tab.

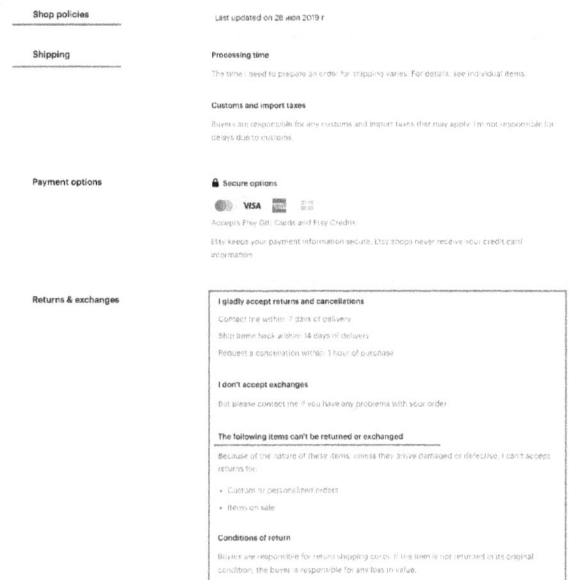

Add sections.

Group your items into categories so shoppers can more easily sift through your products. Much like a navigation bar, the sections will appear on the left side of your home page and will include the number of products within each category. It wouldn't hurt to name them with a keyword, which can index better on search engines on Etsy and even on Google. Like for example here.

All	513
On sale	399
Religious Necklace	53
Animal Necklace	25
Silver Necklace	29
Mythology Necklace	33
Personalized Necklaces	34

STORE CONFIGURATION

Add the "About" section of your shop.

Just like your personal "About" section, your shop also deserves its bio. You have 5,000 characters to tell customers the origin story of your business - keep in mind that Etsy (and customers) value transparency and openness, so don't worry too much about writing traditional marketing copy; be genuine.

Story of SHOPNAME

Jewelry is our family profession. In Istanbul Grand Bazaar, we have worked as production responsible and we have manufactured products to premier brands for years. I was tired of producing products according to others' likings and requests so despite the higher risk of winning less, I have decided to put my own designs into the global market. Now we are ready after hard working over two years in R&D and market reserch. We have created the necessary infrastructure to provide you always the newest models, the fastest delivery system and smoothly products. We are ready for shipping the purchased product in only 1-2 days . Both in purchasing process and after purchasing , we guarantee that we will not compromise our services. Hereby we hope you make the people that you love happy by buying a Bysilverstone design because we have made effort to make you and your favorite people happy and we will continue.

Close

You can also list anyone who helps you produce and create your products or manage your store, provide photos or a video of your studio space or creative process, and add links to your store's social media profiles.

STORE CONFIGURATION

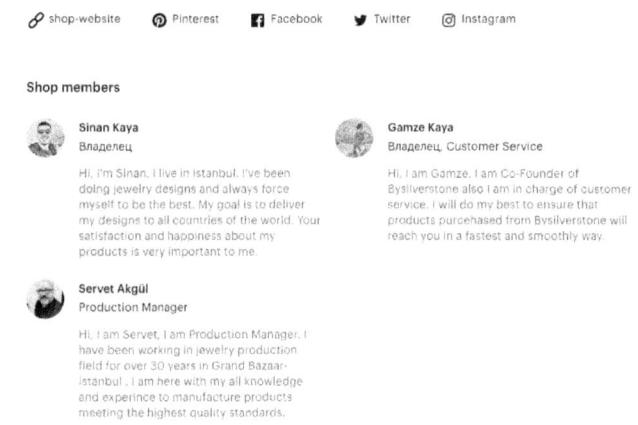

Use Etsy's social media tool.

Advertising your Etsy shop via social media is essential for acquiring new business and keeping your existing base aware of new products.

Luckily, Etsy makes it really easy to do - with the platform's social media tool, you can quickly update all of your social channels with shop announcements, new listings, great reviews, or specific items you want to promote on social media via your phone or the computer. Create the page on Pinterest, Facebook and Instagram with the same name of your shop as on Etsy, to show your competence and professionalism to your customers.

Check.

It is very important to double check everything in your store to see if you have forgotten to add anything. Fill it to the max, let it bring you big profits.

4

Create a professional listing

Okay, we have come this far to know the real secret "how to create a professional listing" that will allow you to tick on the first pages of the search. Read this chapter well, as there are some very delicate and very important moments.

ETSY SEO

SEO - **search engine optimization** (*Search Engine Optimization)* means all those activities aimed at improving the crawling, indexing and positioning of information or content present on a website or in the online store.

How to search for keywords?

There are several tools such as the Google Keyword Planner or the eRank that allow you to identify the most searched keywords.

Let's take an example with the word " **Dog bandana** "On Google Keyword

Planner. It shows you word suggestions, how people search on Google and the monthly amount of requests. Use them correctly with the " **Long Tail Keyword** "Will help you tick in the search better. You will find out how to do it later.

CREATE A PROFESSIONAL LISTING

Keyword	Wed number of requests per month	Competition level	Ad impressions received
The keywords you specified			
dog bandana	10 thousand - 100 thousand	Tall	-
Keyword variations			
dog scarf	1 thousand - 10 thousand	Tall	-
custom dog bandanas	1 thousand - 10 thousand	Tall	-
personalized dog bandanas	1 thousand - 10 thousand	Tall	-
puppy bandanas	1 thousand - 10 thousand	Tall	-
dog birthday bandana	1 thousand - 10 thousand	Tall	-
dog bandana collar	1 thousand - 10 thousand	Tall	-
big brother dog bandana	1 thousand - 10 thousand	Tall	-
dog with bandana	1 thousand - 10 thousand	Middle	-
dog handkerchief	1 thousand - 10 thousand	Tall	-
christmas dog bandanas	1 thousand - 10 thousand	Tall	-
dog cooling bandana	1 thousand - 10 thousand	Tall	-
halloween dog bandana	1 thousand - 10 thousand	Tall	-
bandit bandanas	1 thousand - 10 thousand	Tall	-
dog neckerchief	100 - 1 thous.	Tall	-
big sister dog bandana	100 - 1 thous.	Tall	-

Google Keyword Planner Search

There is also good service, **eRank.com,** which helps you find keywords and shows you how often they are searched, competition and other useful things. This service is free of charge, but there is the possibility of doing a "upgrade" Pro, which will allow you to see more statistics

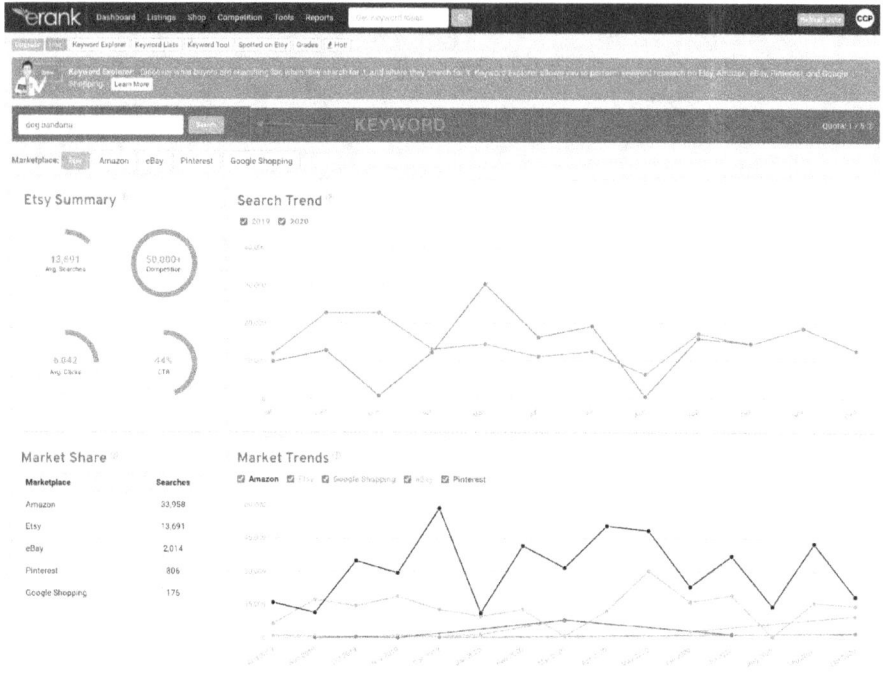

eRank.com statistics

CREATE A PROFESSIONAL LISTING

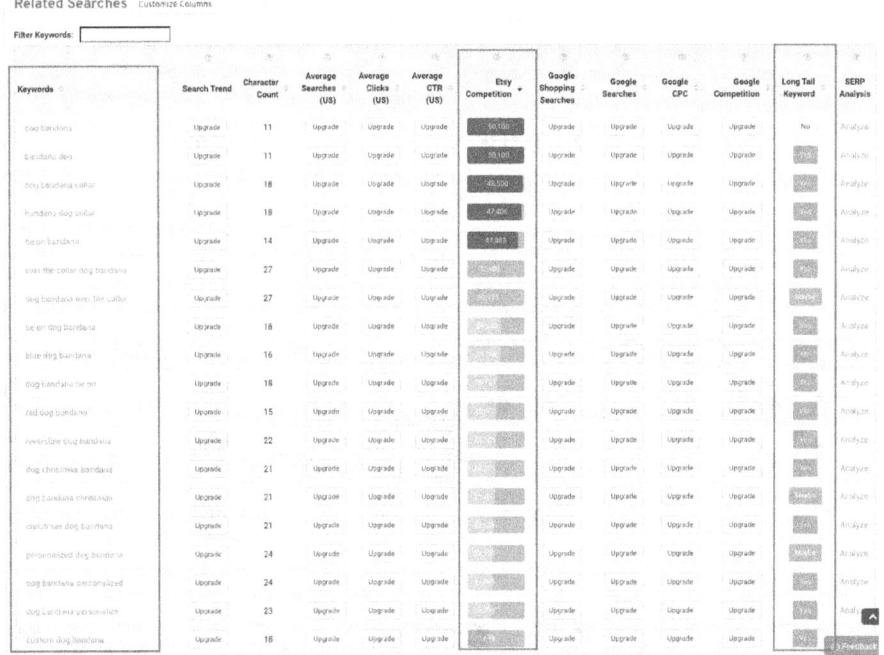

eRank.com keyword tips

The words that have been found here, you can insert in the TAGs, when you create a listing.

Let's move on to research on Etsy now, as there are many interesting tips for our product.

How to write Long Tail Keyword?

On this topic there will be many images to make you understand and explain better.

We always go on with the word "Dog bandana". There are only two words, but a mess in the search results. In total there are 147,524 products with this keyword. If we have just created a listing... bye!

Writing product titles like this is a bad technique, it will get you **ZERO** sales!

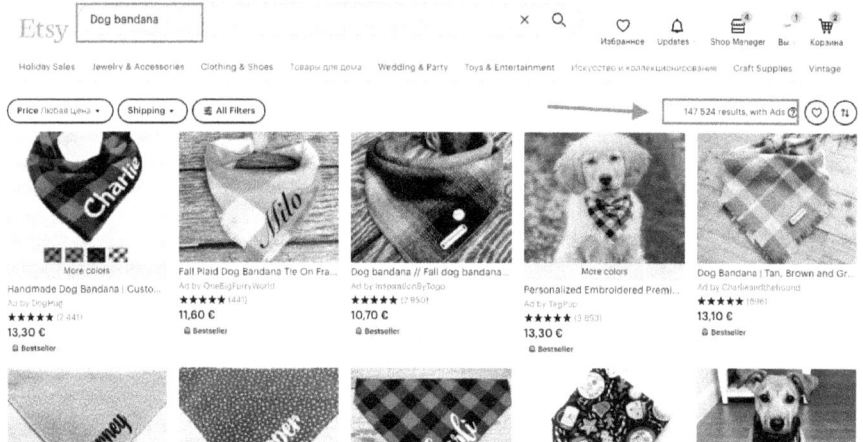

Don't worry. Don't panic. I'm here to teach you how to sell "like a monster".

Put some space in the search, and a window will pop out with more suggestions of the keywords that are used for that product.

CREATE A PROFESSIONAL LISTING

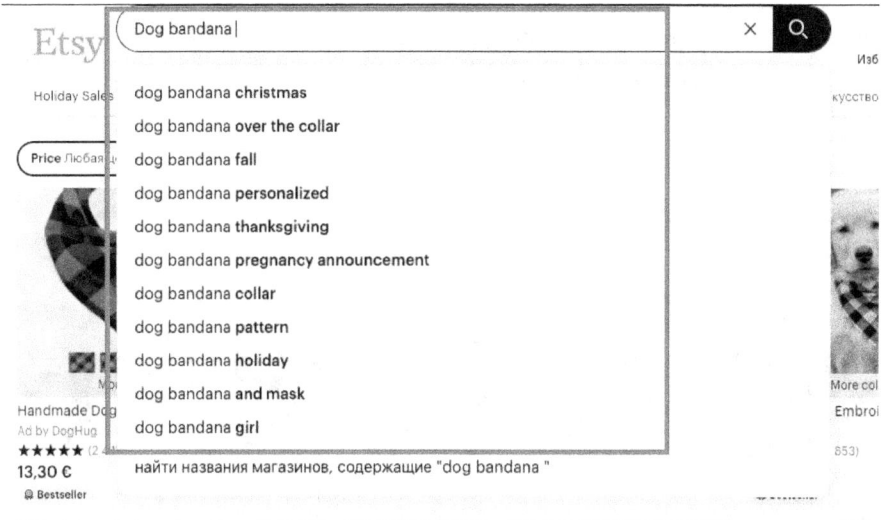

We choose " **customs bandana fall** "First, and then even further" **over collar** ". So our "Long tail keyword" must be " **dog bandana fall over collar** "(Of course if we sell this product).

Now try looking at the search results. Only **3.692** listing. So you are much more likely to sell the products.

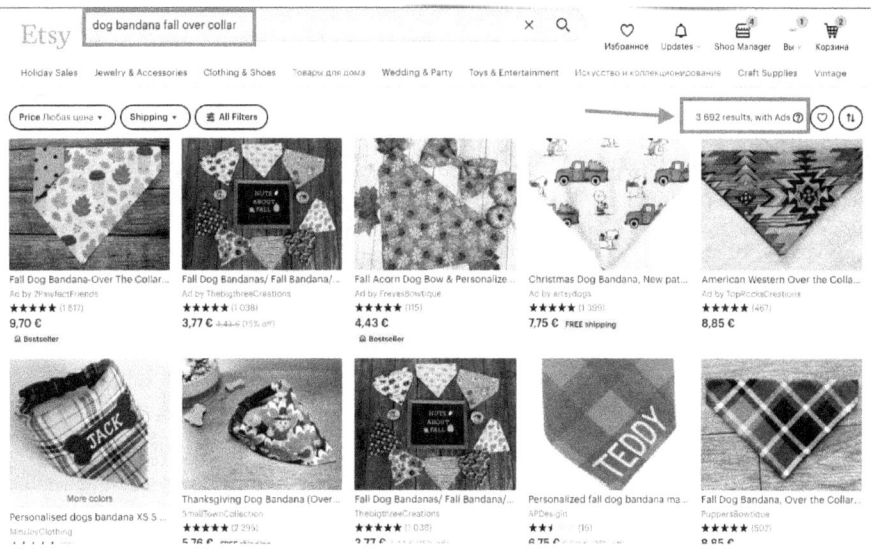

But wait, there are also Filters. Applying the "FREE SHIPPING" filter, ONLY check **117** listing. If you have great quality photos, you steal all sales.

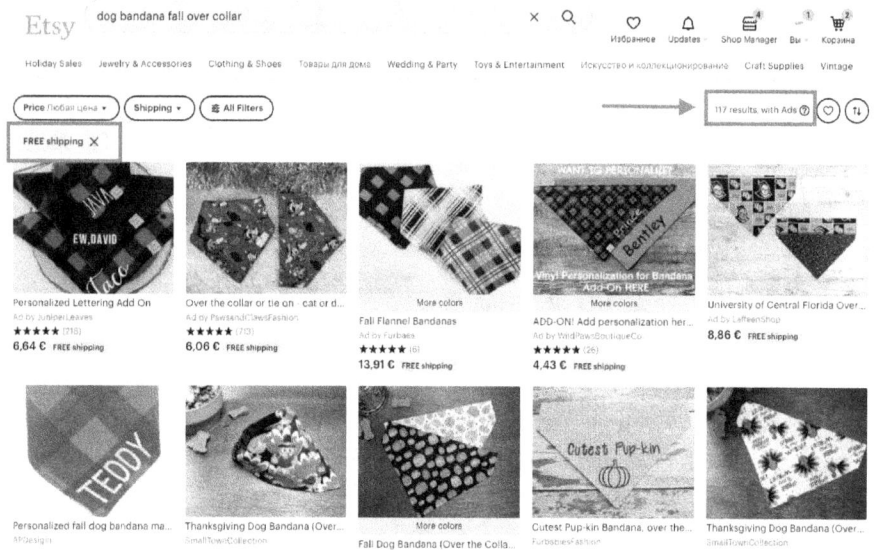

Now let's take another example, short and quick. That sure will be interested many who have a jewelry store.

Let's take for example " **silver pendant** ". When I saw the figure from **2,112,851** listing, I shot a lot of those bad words. Here for sure 100% they will never find you. But to use Etsy ADS (which I'll talk about later) will cost a ton of money for just one click… which isn't worth it at all.

CREATE A PROFESSIONAL LISTING

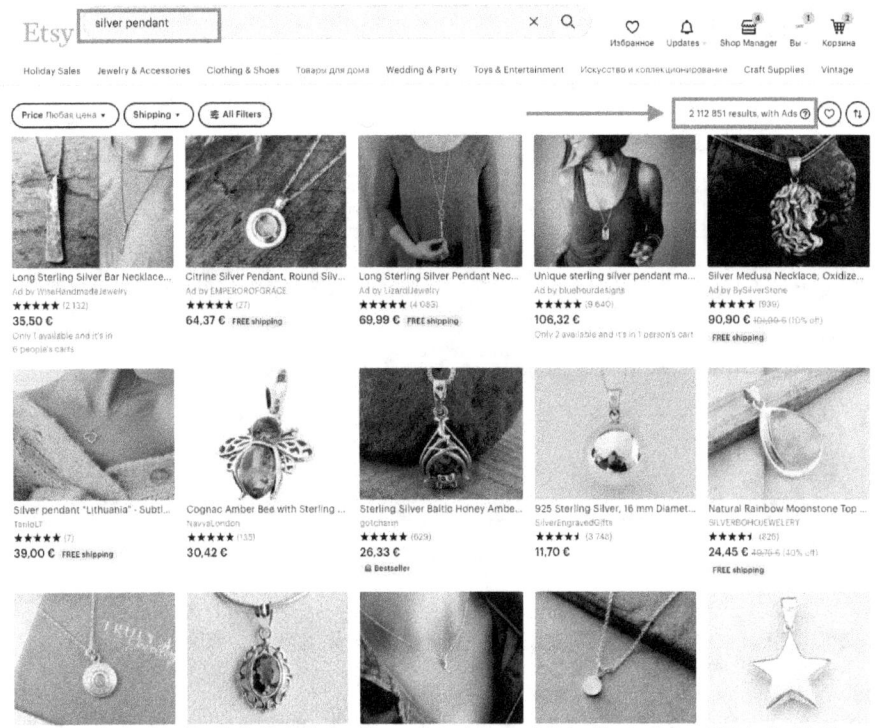

We extend the word " **silver pendant necklace dainty eye** "And we apply

a couple of filters like " **shipping 1-3 days** "," **Free delivery** ",

" **Discount** ". Now from 2 million we are at only 106 results. Your sales will blow up. At the end I will explain the WINNING technique to be on top

1.

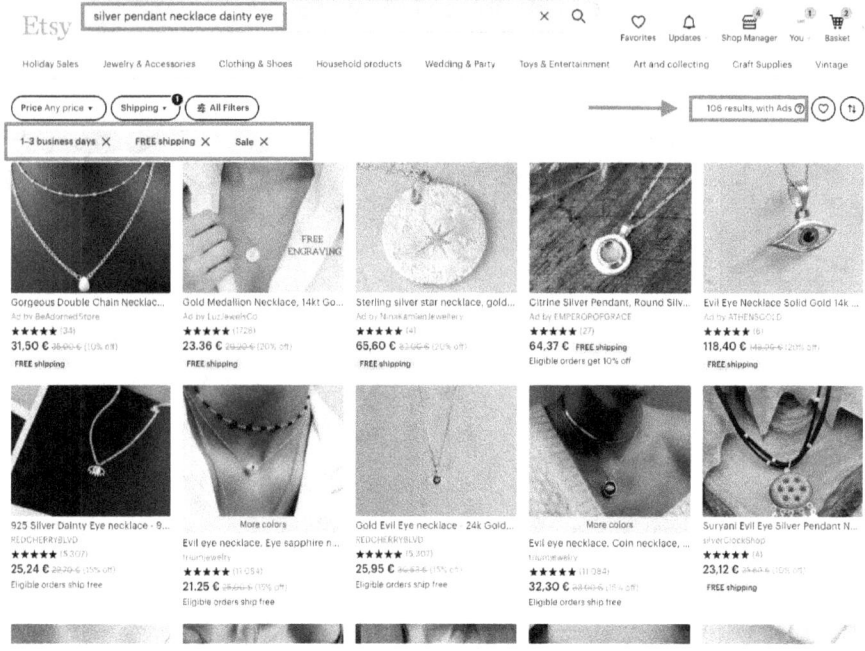

So, as we understand, when you create the listing, the title must be Long Tail. You basically have to describe your product in 3-5 words.

One more example. If you sell the wall clock, that would be " **clock wall** "As the main keyword, but after you have to describe it so that you can be found faster by those words.

CREATE A PROFESSIONAL LISTING

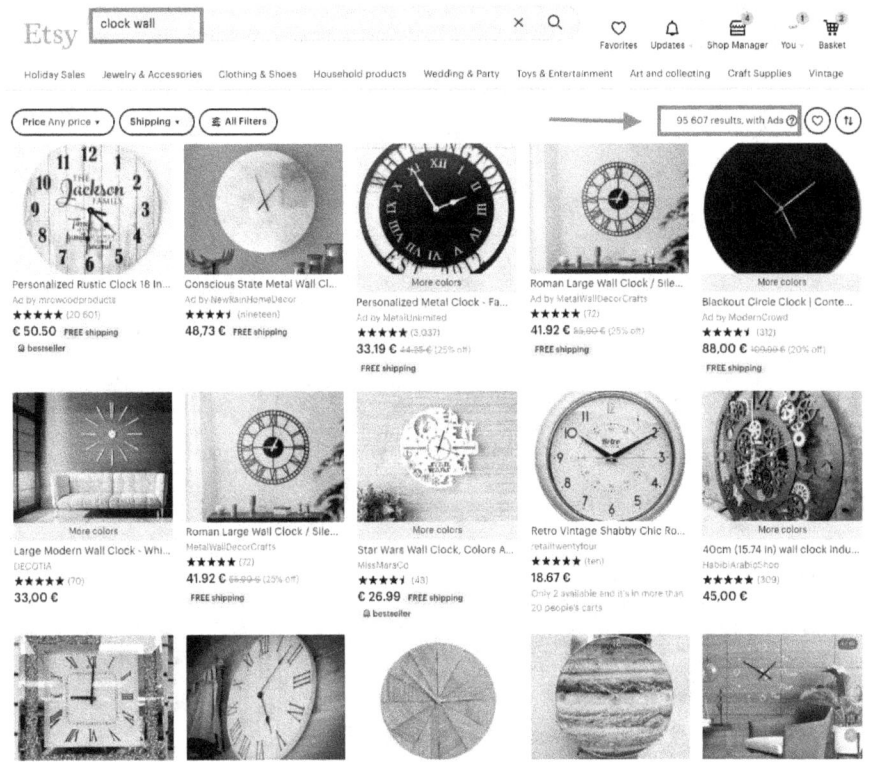

As you can see, there are 95,607 other products with this word, but if your epoxy resin watch is blue in color, you have to write " **clock wall epoxy resin blue** ". We stopped at only 251 results, so as I said

- for sure you will have sales.

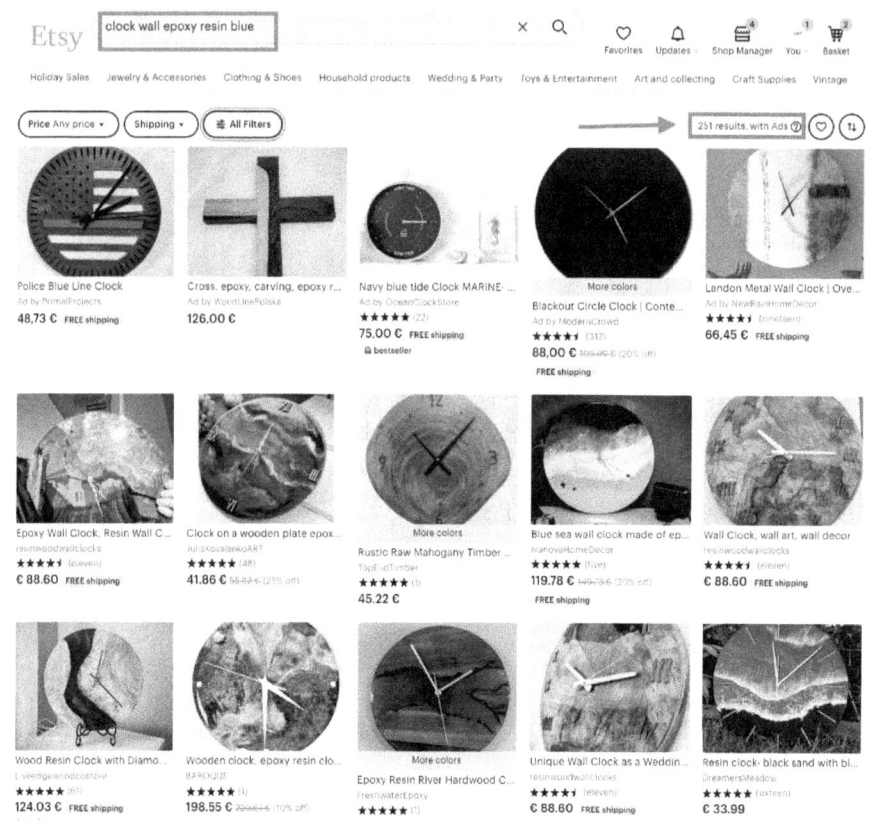

One thing though, describe the title with 3 or 4 pieces of long tail keyword. That is:

" **clockwall epoxy resin blue, epoxy resin bluewall clock, blue clock for wall epoxy resin for kids** ". This is a perfect title to get found faster and build a lot of sales.

Conclusion: Define keywords for your title in the Etsy + search coffin by adding the words about your product. It must be 3-4 long tails... more - even better. Using Google Keyword Planner and eRank, you can find keywords to insert in TAGs.

CREATE A PROFESSIONAL LISTING

The photos. How should they be?

This is a global problem for most stores. About 95% of the shops have terrible photos of poor quality and small quantities. Many years of practice and experience I give you some great advice. Take product photos of roughly the same colors and background.

Example 1

All Items

Jesus Crucifix Necklace, Christ Jesu...
111,60 € 124,00 € (10% off)
FREE shipping

Solid Silver Jesus Head Necklace, M...
111,60 € 124,00 € (10% off)
FREE shipping

Archangel Saint Michael Silver Meda...
111,60 € 124,00 € (10% off)
FREE shipping

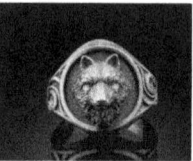
Mens Silver Wolf Ring, Wolf Head M...
96,30 € 107,00 € (10% off)
FREE shipping

Personalized 14K Solid Gold Lion Me...
576,00 € FREE shipping
16 people have this in their cart

Silver Crucifix Mens Necklace, Amer...
111,60 € 124,00 € (10% off)
FREE shipping

Silver Saint George Mens Necklace, ...
111,60 € 124,00 € (10% off)
FREE shipping

14K Solid Gold Personalized Lion Ne...
621,00 € FREE shipping
6 people have this in their cart

Winged Lion Silver Men's Ring, Oval ...
87,67 € 97,40 € (10% off)
FREE shipping

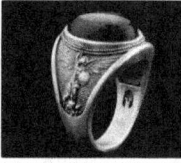
Archangel Saint Michael Silver Men ...
87,67 € 97,40 € (10% off)
FREE shipping

Silver Ecce Homo Men Necklace, Ec...
111,60 € 124,00 € (10% off)
FREE shipping

10K Solid Gold Lion Mens Ring, Sign...
514,00 € FREE shipping
13 people have this in their cart

10K Solid Gold Mens Ring, Gemston...
643,00 € FREE shipping

Saint Christopher Necklace, Mens St...
111,60 € 124,00 € (10% off)
FREE shipping

Men Dragon Necklace, Unisex Silver ...
104,40 € 116,00 € (10% off)
FREE shipping

Silver Jesus Sacred Heart Mens Nec...
111,60 € 124,00 € (10% off)
FREE shipping

Example 2

Beautiful, is not it? I think you understand what I mean. Several shops, but the same idea. Find yourself in a permanent place to take photos on the same background. I recommend learning to use some apps to add saturation and color to your photos. For this it would be fine **Adobe Lightroom.**

Show customers the product from different sides and how they look if they are worn.

CREATE A PROFESSIONAL LISTING

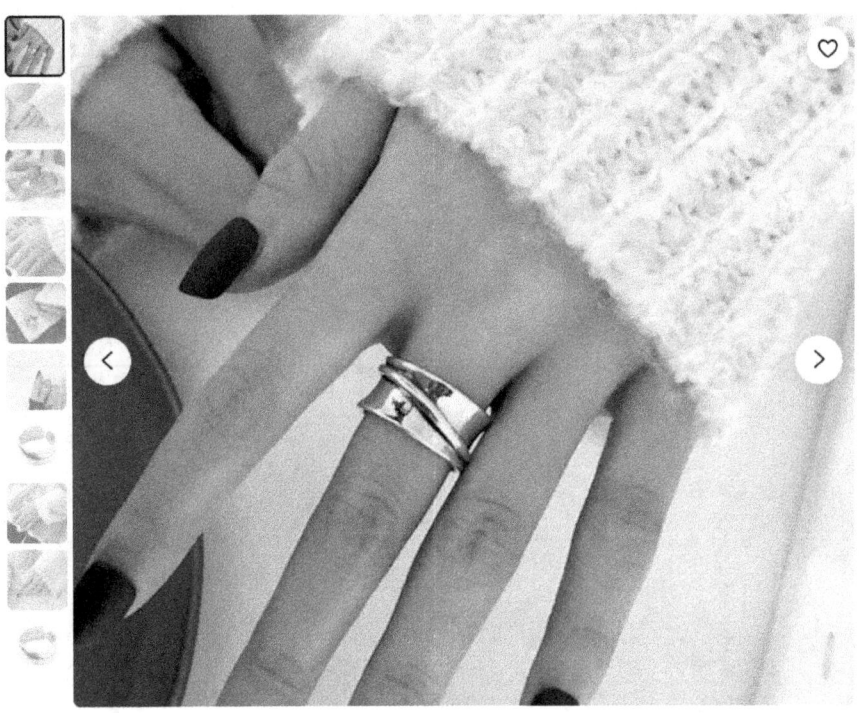

THE ART OF ETSY.

← Back to search results

CREATE A PROFESSIONAL LISTING

Add as many photos as possible, as Etsy will show you more in the search. Now you can also upload a short video of the product, which will just blow up your sales.

Parameters and material

Add all necessary parameters related to your product to make it better and easier for shoppers to navigate and for greater search relevance. What does this product consist of? What color is it? Which size? How much does it weight?. This is all very, very important, because Etsy takes this into account in the search query.

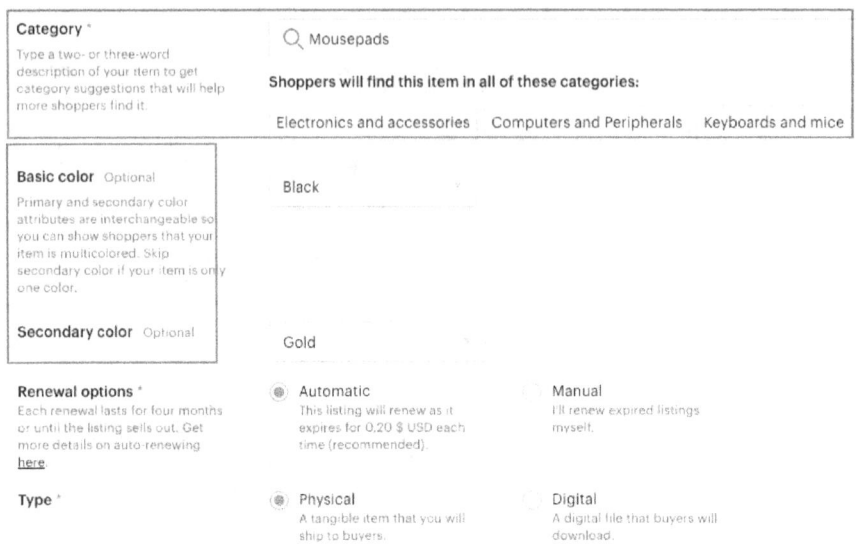

Description

Describe your product from A to Z.

How to write a description? Put your product in front of you, describe it, what sensations it gives, what quality it is, what it consists of, how to use it. **Nonetheless- care the keywords we searched for earlier.** They must be in the description, this is very important.

Add all other parameters related to your product. Write the dimensions in centimeters / millimeters and the weight in kilograms / grams and pounds, for customers not only from the United States, but also for Europe and other countries of the world.

Sections

Add your product to different sections (if you have one). If you sell clothes: sweaters, t-shirts, trousers, for men and women - the sections are mandatory. They will also play a role in search and improve navigation for customers.

Section Optional — Anime

Tag

We've talked about this before. These are the keywords to find your product. Using eRank and Google Keyword Planner, you'll define what they do for you. The first 3-5 tags are most important. Enter the ones with best ratio **CTR / low competition.** Remember that you have to write all 13.

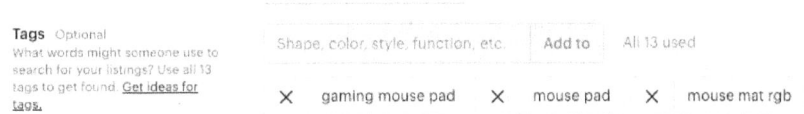

Price

Evaluate your product, how much it can cost and how much you would pay for it yourself. It is not necessary to stoop to too high and not too low a price. We must sell at a profit and not at a loss. We are here to do business and make money.

Shipment

Let the customer know where the product is being shipped from, how long it takes to process the order, and how long the delivery will take.

Processing time *

Once purchased, how long does it take you to ship an item?

1-3 business days

Anywhere in the world   Shipping carrier   Delivery time Business days

Other   4   12

What you'll charge

Free shipping

Create a "Shipping profile" to not enter the same thing every time. How do you? Very simple, go on **Settings -> Shipping Settings -> Shipping Profiles.**

Conclusion: The best strategy for getting more customers and being first in search is: ***order processing 1-3 days (but it depends on your product and how long it takes to create it), delivery time 4 to 13 days, free shipping.***

CREATE A PROFESSIONAL LISTING

Processing time *

Once purchased, how long does it take you to ship an item?

1-3 business days

Buyers are more likely to purchase items that ship quickly

Fixed shipping prices *   Only shoppers in countries you ship to will see your listings in search.

Standard shipping

Italy	Shipping carrier ⓘ	Delivery time Business days
	Other	3 - 13
	What you'll charge	
	Free shipping	

Everywhere Else	Shipping carrier ⓘ	Delivery time Business days
	Other	4 - 13
	What you'll charge	
	Free shipping	

5

Etsy Marketing

In this chapter, we will review and analyze some of the Etsy marketing points you should and shouldn't use.

Etsy Ads

Etsy ads can be useful for promoting your product by high frequency keywords, but the cost per click can be too high, which means you will spend more on advertising than your product.
will pay. There are other cases where the **advertising can earn you dozens and hundreds of thousands of dollars.** It will show you to customers in the top end of the search with very "heavy" keywords that result in 2,117,118 products.

ETSY MARKETING

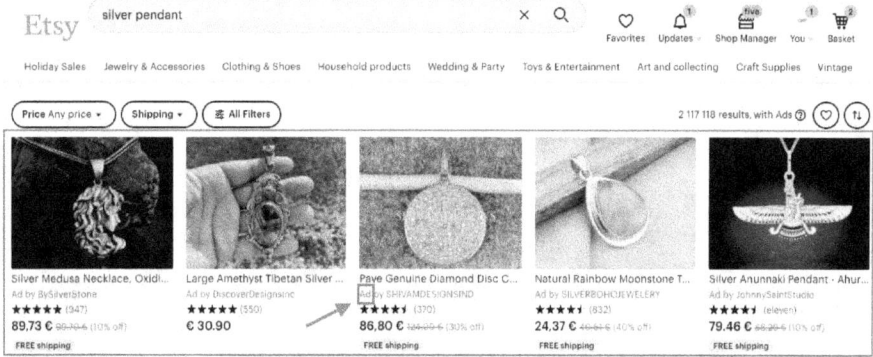

Sales and Coupon

Make a discount for all Etsy shoppers or just your current customers.

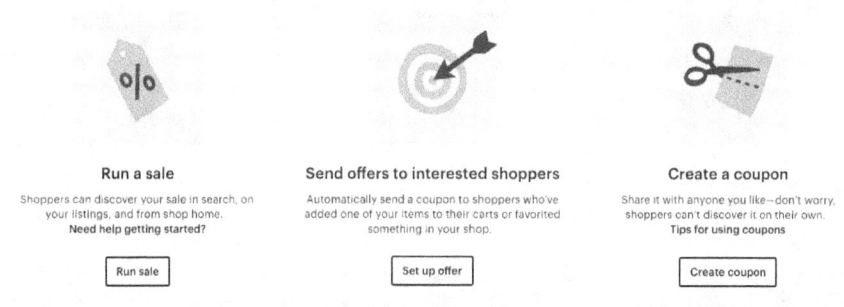

It will be a good experience to make a discount on all products with a minimum percentage of 10% so that your product appears better in the search. But don't forget to add 10% to the current price of your product so you can make money. Everyone loves discounts, so keep this strategy in mind and you'll have a lot of sales.

I'd like to offer shoppers... How much of a discount should I offer?	Percentage off	10% off
Where is this offer valid? You can set a sale to be valid for a specific country.	Everywhere	
Minimum order to qualify When should I set a minimum?	● None Quantity	Order total
Duration Sales can run up to 30 days. Consider running sales around these key shopping dates.	15.11.2020	29.11.2020
Terms and conditions (optional) If your sale has restrictions, limitations, or other terms you want to make shoppers aware of, list them here. Shoppers will see these on eligible listings for the duration of your sale.		500 characters remaining
Name your sale Shoppers won't see this name, but it's how you'll track its performance. Each sale needs a unique name, and can only contain letters and numbers.	XMASS10	

Let's see a small example, like with 2 million products, **applying a discount in the filters,** you can move very quickly in the search, removing 1 million and 600 thousand other products.

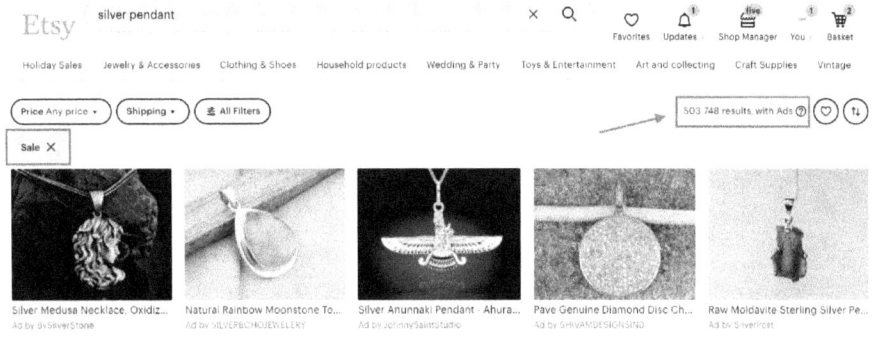

Conclusion: The discount for product promotion plays a very important role. Use this strategy.

6

What to do if my first order has arrived?

- Ship it!

- Oh yes? Thanks cap.

 Orders & Shipping   832

Prepare your package for shipment, write the address from where and where. You can find the address in the orders. I advise you to check the correctness of the address in Google MAPS, it happens that the customer may not write it correctly and if we send the goods to the wrong place - we will be very sorry, because we will have to return the money to the customer and we are left without the goods. Also, the customer may leave us a bad review due to our lack of professionalism. If in the end we discover that the address is wrong or is different from that of the order, we contact the customer and ask to write it correctly.

Try to confirm the shipment within those 1-3 days (if you entered these in the " **Shipping Profile** "), To avoid annoying questions from the customer regarding his order.

Conclusion: I recommend contacting the customer, thank them for this order, kindly ask for the phone number to put it on the package, as the courier may be incompetent to find the address, and may telephone the customer.

II

Part Two

In the second part of this book, we will look at how to communicate with customers, how to handle disputes, how not to infringe on copyrights, successful strategies and shops and how much they make.

7

Drop Shipping

This hour will be useful for those who are busy or want to get involved in this type of business.

Is dropshipping allowed on Etsy? It's hard to answer, if we use the strategy correctly, we won't get caught by Etsy - success will await us. The strategy has some nuances though.

Let's see a strategy.

1. We decide in which niche we want to sell.
2. We are looking for such a product on Aliexpress.
3. We order to "orders" so that before we are assigned the most sold.

4. Checking the product trend on Google Trends _____
5. We search for keywords based on the strategy we have defined previously.

6. We order one by one from our supplier to check the quality.
7. If we are satisfied, we take quality photos and order other different products. (No need to buy in bulk)
8. Create a product listing on Etsy, as we wrote in the chapter
    4.

9. Start selling while more products are delivered to take pictures.

10. When you get an order on Etsy, you go to your supplier's Aliexpress, and create the order for that product, but enter the address of the customer who ordered from you on Etsy.

11. Profit!

Simple.

ps If you need help with Etsy sales, we offer our shop management services that will earn you not $ 1,000, not $ 5,000,

not even $ *10,000* nor $ *15,000* per month, but you can get around $ *30,000* and even more with sales. The figure seems laughable, but trust us, that some customers of our services **they earn $ 50,000 a month.**

8

Manage customers.

If you are a strict, nervous and short-tempered person in life. Remember, on etsy and in the sales industry, you have to be nice to customers, without " **ou uncle,
you broke ..., this M *** A order will arrive soon!** ", Because customers do you
they pay. If you can't cope with that task, ask another person to communicate with customers.

Calm down and relax, life is great, sell, earn and do business. Always reply to customer emails, answer their questions. You can't now, answer as soon as possible. Customers want attention. At the end of the message always write: your name, name of the shop and "Thanks and Best Regards".

> *Sergio Maley, CEO of **www.sergiomaley.com** (* or the name of the shop)
> *Thank You and Best Regards :)*

When you reply to messages - laugh, always laugh. A smile will positively influence your customer through a message as well. If you're nervous, you can write bad words, then get offended, want a refund, and leave you a bad review. And this will greatly affect your sales and the future of your store as a whole.

Be positive and there will be positive sales. **Remember this.**

9

Manage disputes

No matter how well you sell, no matter how many sales you have, there will always be a customer who is dissatisfied with something: service, quality of goods, speed of delivery, attitude. Sooner or later someone will open a case against your store.

How to handle disputes?

First, we need to understand why he opened this controversy, what was the reason? Product quality? Or was the item not delivered?

If this is quality, as I wrote before, **we must check the quality of our product,** include quality details in the description. If the dispute is open, then it will be possible to respond by saying that it was in the product description, but the customer did not read it, so we will win the dispute and not have to return the money. If you leave the negative review, we can open the dispute regarding the negative review by explaining that we don't deserve this review because the customer paid little attention, and Etsy will delete it.

If the product was electronic and has stopped working, within a certain number of days the customer must contact us, return the product, after verification by us, we decide whether to refund the money or send another product.

If the item has not arrived on time, this is our responsibility, as we have chosen the courier with whom to ship.

We check on the courier's official website the tracking number where the package is, if it is still on the way, we must apologize, explain the situation and tell him it will arrive soon. If the code turns out nothing and is lost ... there is nothing we can do but refund the money. **Remember that the customer is always right.** I recommend that you ship your packages with a tracking number and put on Etsy when confirming an order.

10

Copyright infringement

It is absolutely forbidden to sell counterfeit products or products that violate the right of ownership. If you want to sell paintings with Harry Potter or other characters from the films, you should not make a copy super exact, and not to write it in the title or description, you can write **ONLY** in tags.

What could happen?

Sooner or later, one fine morning, when you wake up, have breakfast, do your housework, you will notice on your phone that you are not receiving order notifications, by logging into your account, you will find this wonderful message " **Your account is suspended** ". The first thing you will do - you start swearing, but a lot though.

Don't worry, this problem can be solved. We need to write to Etsy, explain the situation, if we know that somehow and somewhere we may be infringing rights, then we promise not to do it again (and we actually don't anymore). It happens that even if you have not violated the rights, you can find this message, but this is due to errors in the algorithm on Etsy, which sometimes fail in the system.

The right to make mistakes is granted only once. There next time, they may not unlock the shop and permanently block our access to Etsy sales. Be very careful what you sell. Don't look at other vendors selling Deadpool's products this open, sooner or later they'll find that message (if they don't have the right to sell that product, they may have asked Marvel's permission).

What can they block for?

For example, if you sell paintings with famous people, Etsy will first delete this listing by sending you a notice, after 3-4 such notices it will block your shop. If you get the first such notice, think about what you are selling.

You are given a great opportunity to sell a lot and earn even more. Don't waste this opportunity.

11

Winning strategy.

The time has come to write one of the strategies for $ 50,000 per month, $ 600,000 per year and $ 6,000,000 over 10 years.

The strategy.

1. **The shop at the beginning as our niche eg.** "AnimeStick-ersShop ".
2. **All that in chapter 3.**
3. **All that in Chapter 4.**
4. Create the discount (10%) for your products, which in this way will be more visible in the search.
5. **Create free shipping. (if you don't fit in, enter the shipping price you have to pay in the product price).**
6. **Order processing 1-3 days.**

Why in point 2 and 3 did I send you again to read chapters 3 and 4? **Because they are very important!** reread them, learn them as "Our Father". There are so many points you need to hook and put them into practice.

See how the dates change by putting simple 3 things in the filter. From 2 million, we went to 80,000.

THE ART OF ETSY.

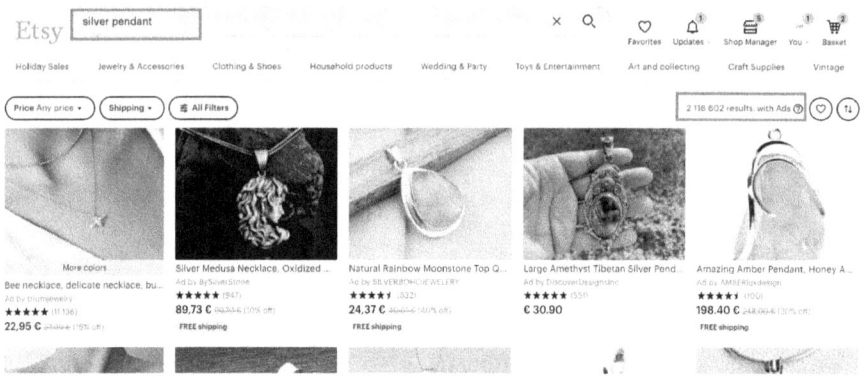

And you think that these are just some filters, but there are many others. That's why I told you to learn chapters 3 and 4. To enter all the necessary data.

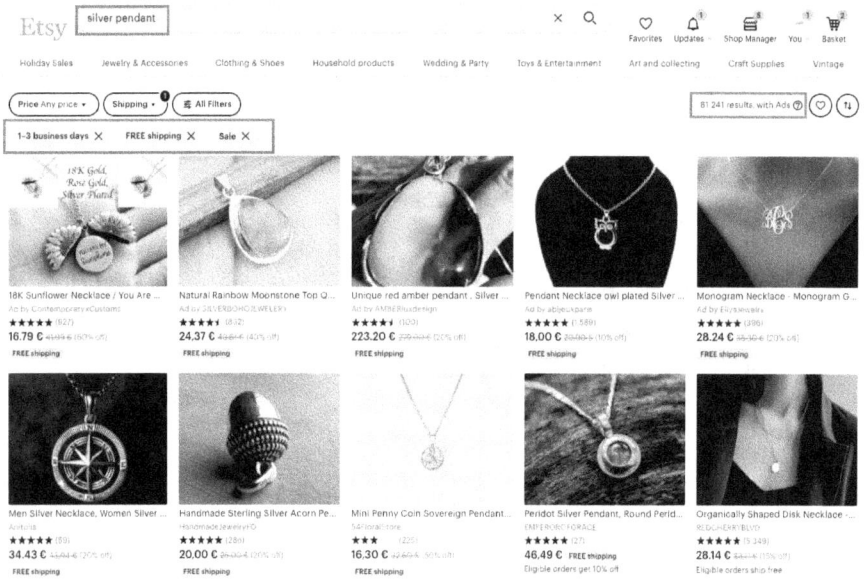

Use the strategy. Sell a lot. But if you can't or don't want to because you are lazy, we offer you our services for the Audit, management and arrangement of your shop on Etsy, which you will not be able to keep up with your orders to ship, because there is and there will be so many that you will pray to God to help you.

12

Success Stories

In this chapter, I want to encourage you to study this book better and better. Here I will give you five examples of other stores, how they have made lists… and the most interesting - how much they have earned during their existence.

BySilverStone

A jewelry store, with 4,269 (current) sales, and an average price of € 534. It has existed since 2018. Up to now it has earned € 2,279,646. So per month they are around € 94,985.

THE ART OF ETSY.

BySilverStone

Rings, Necklaces, Pendants, Chains, Medallions and more

On Etsy since 2018

4 269 Sales ★★★★★

♡ Favorite shop (2828)

Buyers are raving! This shop got multiple 5-star reviews in the past 7 days.

SHOP OWNER

Sinan Kaya
✉ Contact

Items

Sort: Ascending prices ▾

Search items 🔍	
All	512
Religious Necklace	53
Animal Necklace	25
Silver Necklace	29
Mythology Necklace	33
Personalized Necklaces	34
Gold Necklace	40
Chain Necklaces	nineteen
Signet Ring	45

Round Signet Mens Ring, Me...
751,00 € FREE shipping

3 people have this in their cart

18K Solid Gold Gorilla Men's ...
751,00 € FREE shipping

18K Gold Men Square Ring, ...
751,00 € FREE shipping

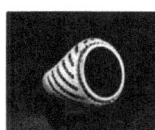
Gold Signet Oval Ring, Onyx ...
751,00 € FREE shipping

14K Gold Men Ring, Signet G...

751,00 € FREE shipping

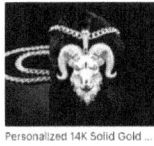
Personalized 14K Solid Gold ...
808,00 € FREE shipping

14K Solid Gold Compass Me...

813,00 € FREE shipping

Personalized 14K Solid Gold ...
1,010.00 € FREE shipping
4 people have this in their cart

DigitalPlannerTools

This shop deals with digital planner (and not only). There are currently 12,690 sales with an average price € 20.99. It has existed since 2019 and in all that time it has earned around € 266,363. Not bad. Do you agree?

SUCCESS STORIES

ShopLuminJewelry

Another jewelry store with 12,118 sales and an average price of € 51.50. It exists since 2015 and its earnings are approximately € 624,077. Try earning that money by working in the company ...

THE ART OF ETSY.

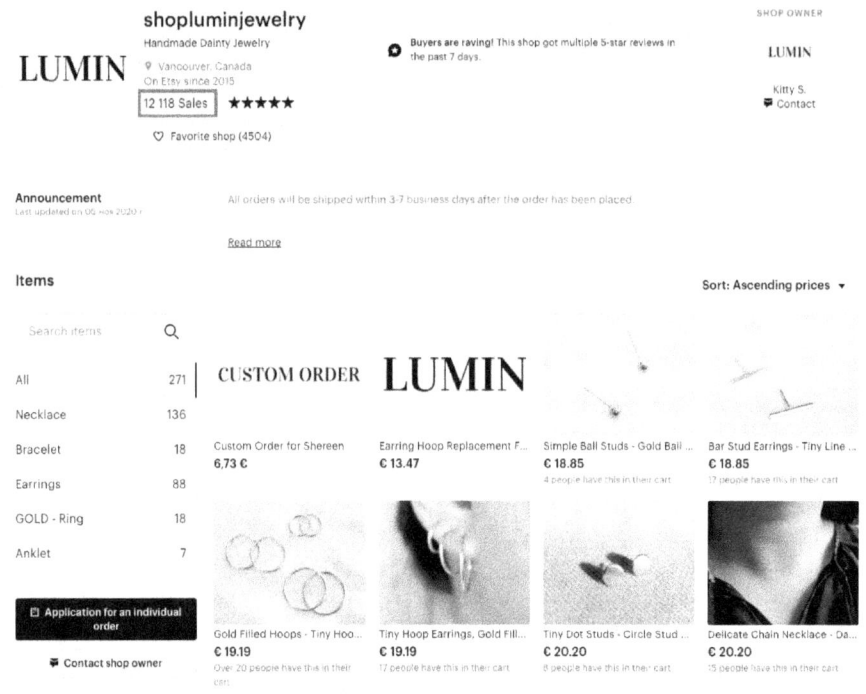

85thAdventureDesigns

A shop for clothes and stickers (for clothes and other items). It has existed since 2017 and has sold the stuff for 39,369, with an average price of € 18.05. His earnings will be roughly € 710,610. In just 3 years ...

SUCCESS STORIES

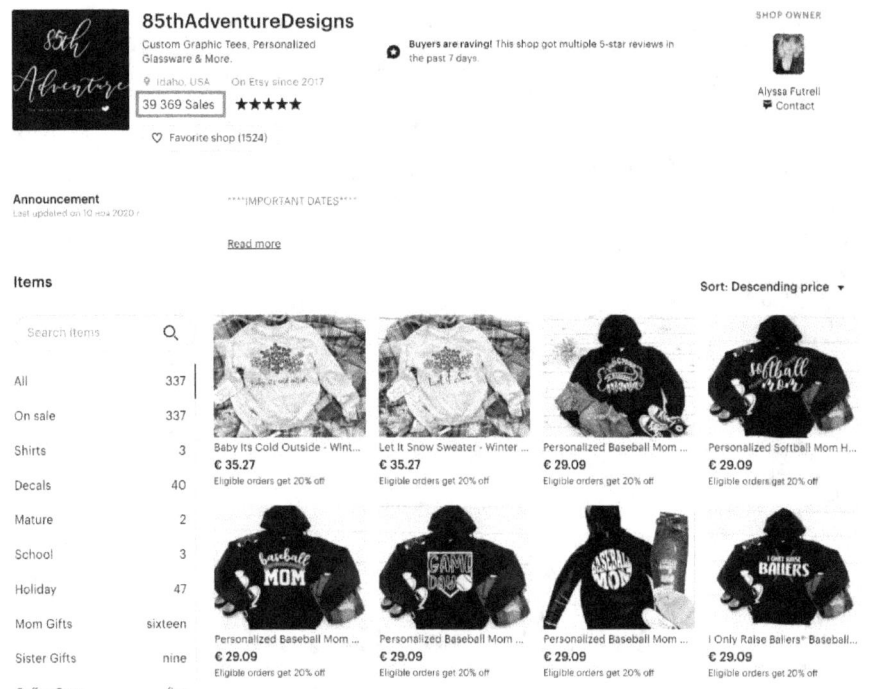

StoneCreekWallDecals

A shop with wall decorations. It exists since 2012 and there are 26,255 current sales at an average price around € 30.02. In 8 years he earned € 788,175. Great I'd say. That money, being a bartender or metalworker, you will not see it. We will be honest with ourselves.

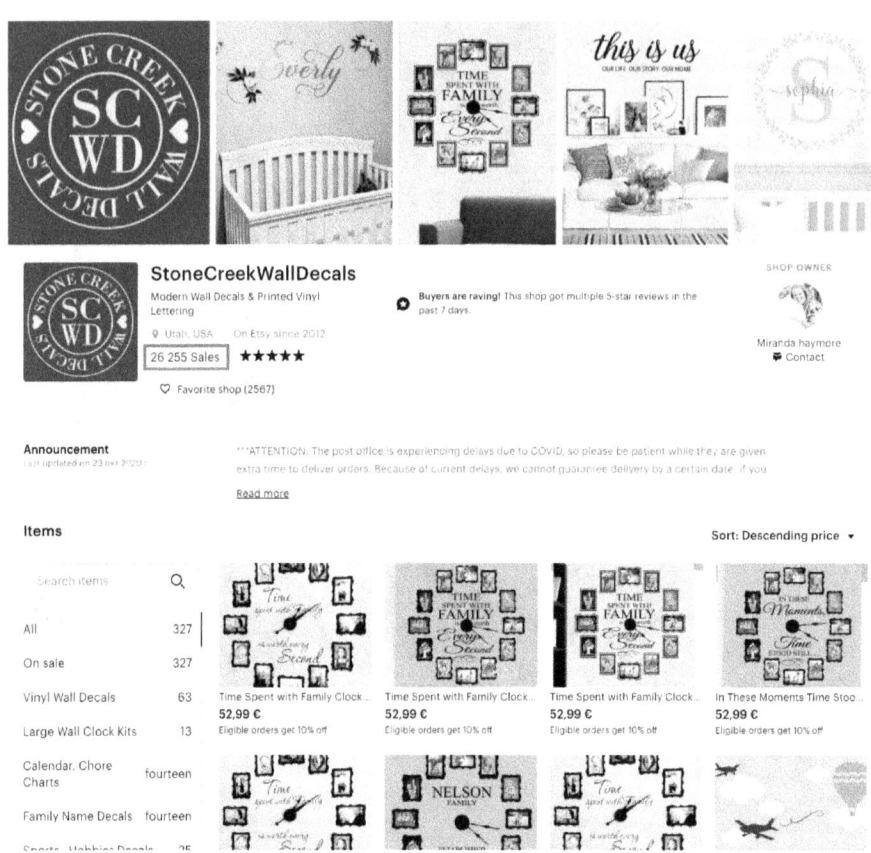

So we went through some store stories and as you can see, everything works. On Etsy you can earn a lot of money by working with pleasure and for yourself. But for that you have to work on the shop and yourself first, so that you learn the art of selling on Etsy.

These are the shops that work with a clear strategy, know how to write keywords and know how to sell. Use this book as a guide, like a Bible. Read it and study it.

If you have any questions or need help, please contact me on **www.sergiomaley.com**.
Follow me also on instagram: @ *sergio.maley*

SUCCESS STORIES

Sales be with you.

About the Author

I live in Italy, but I come from Ukraine. Many years of studying web technologies and web marketing. Managing e-commerce, writing promotional articles, and setting up targeted ads. Investing in the stock market. I like to read books, and I speak six languages.

You can connect with me on:
- https://www.sergiomaley.com
- https://www.facebook.com/xSpesheRx
- https://www.instagram.com/sergio.maley

Subscribe to my newsletter:
- https://www.sergiomaley.com

Also by Sergio Maley

Must have for sellers.

The art of Etsy

Sell like a monster. **SEO, Marketing, Copywriting, Winning Strategies, Success Stories. Anything to blow your Etsy sales.**

www.ingramcontent.com/pod-product-compliance
Lightning Source LLC
Chambersburg PA
CBHW070453220526
45466CB00004B/1816